Manatee coloring b... ts

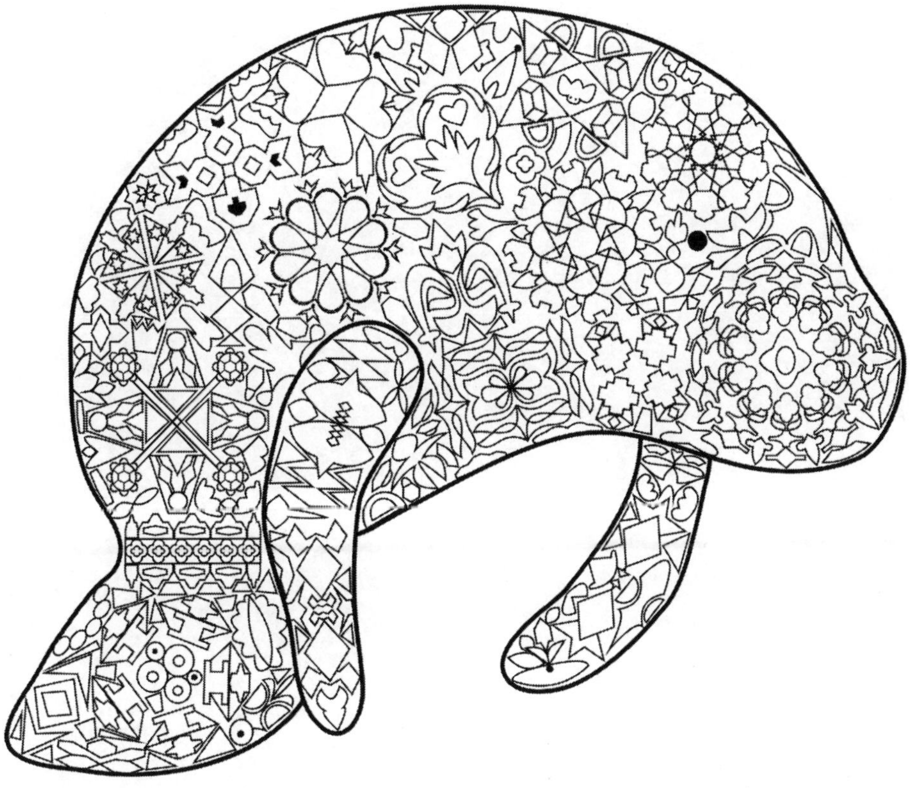

ISBN-13: 978-1974692712

ISBN-10: 197469271X

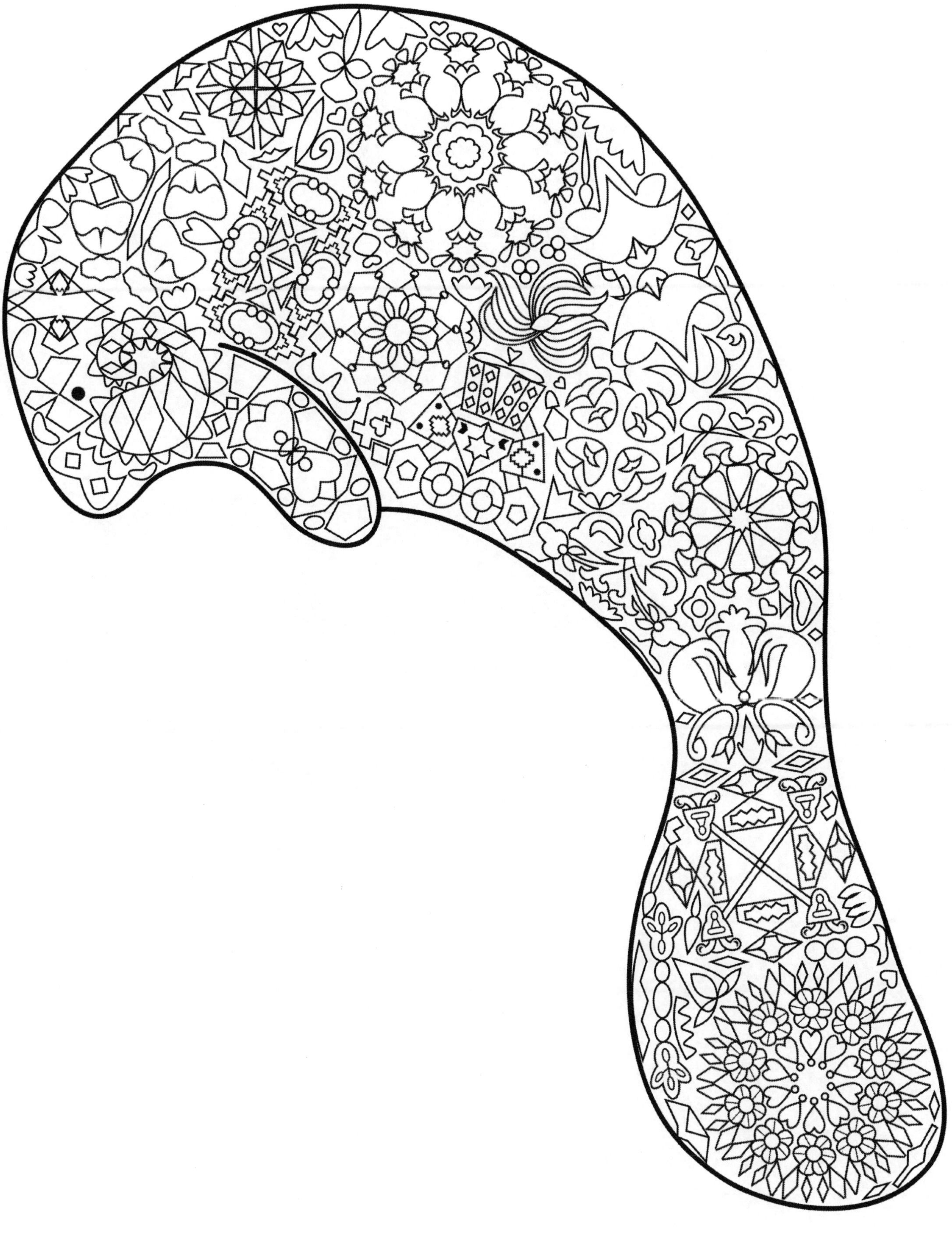

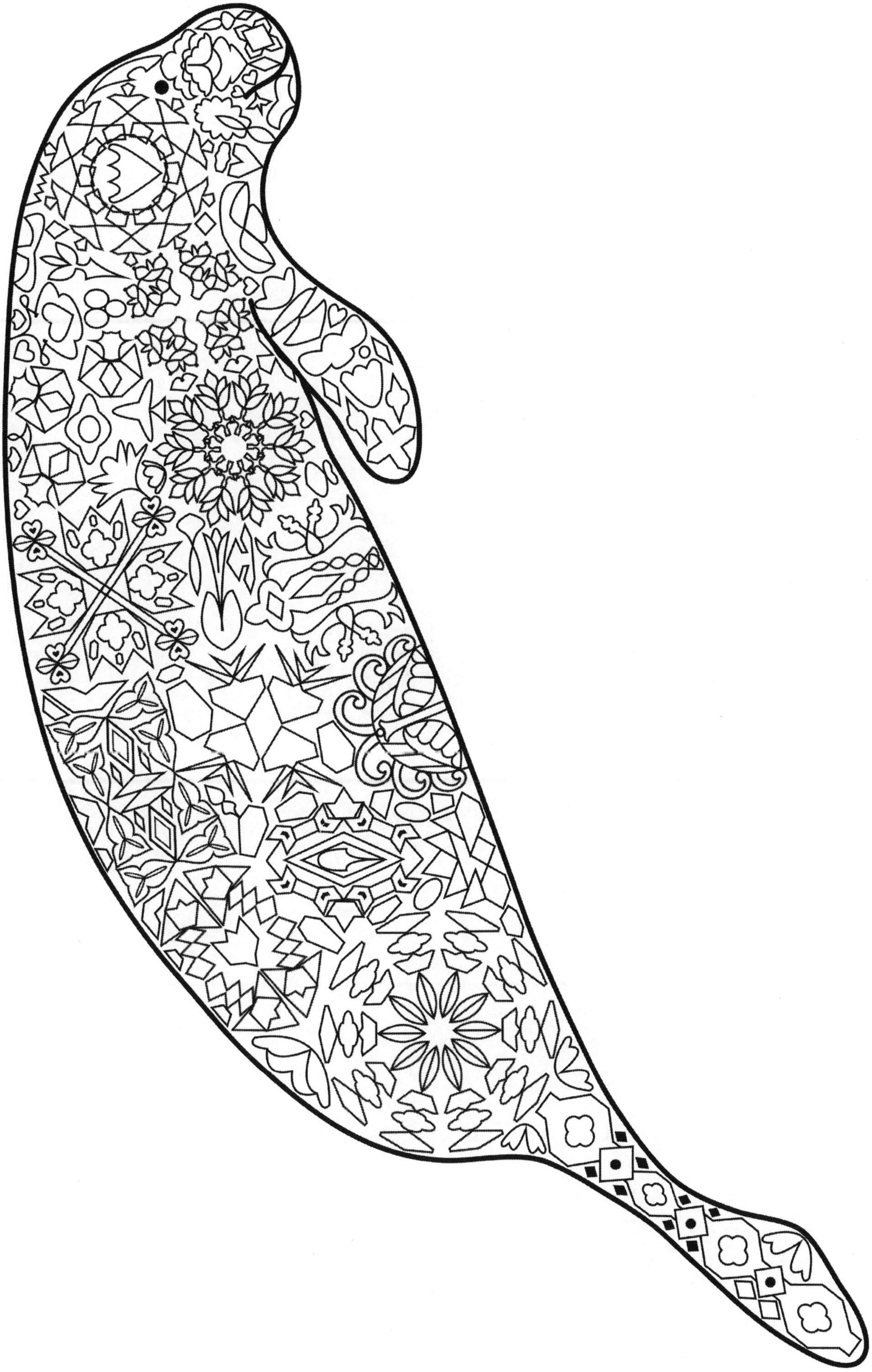

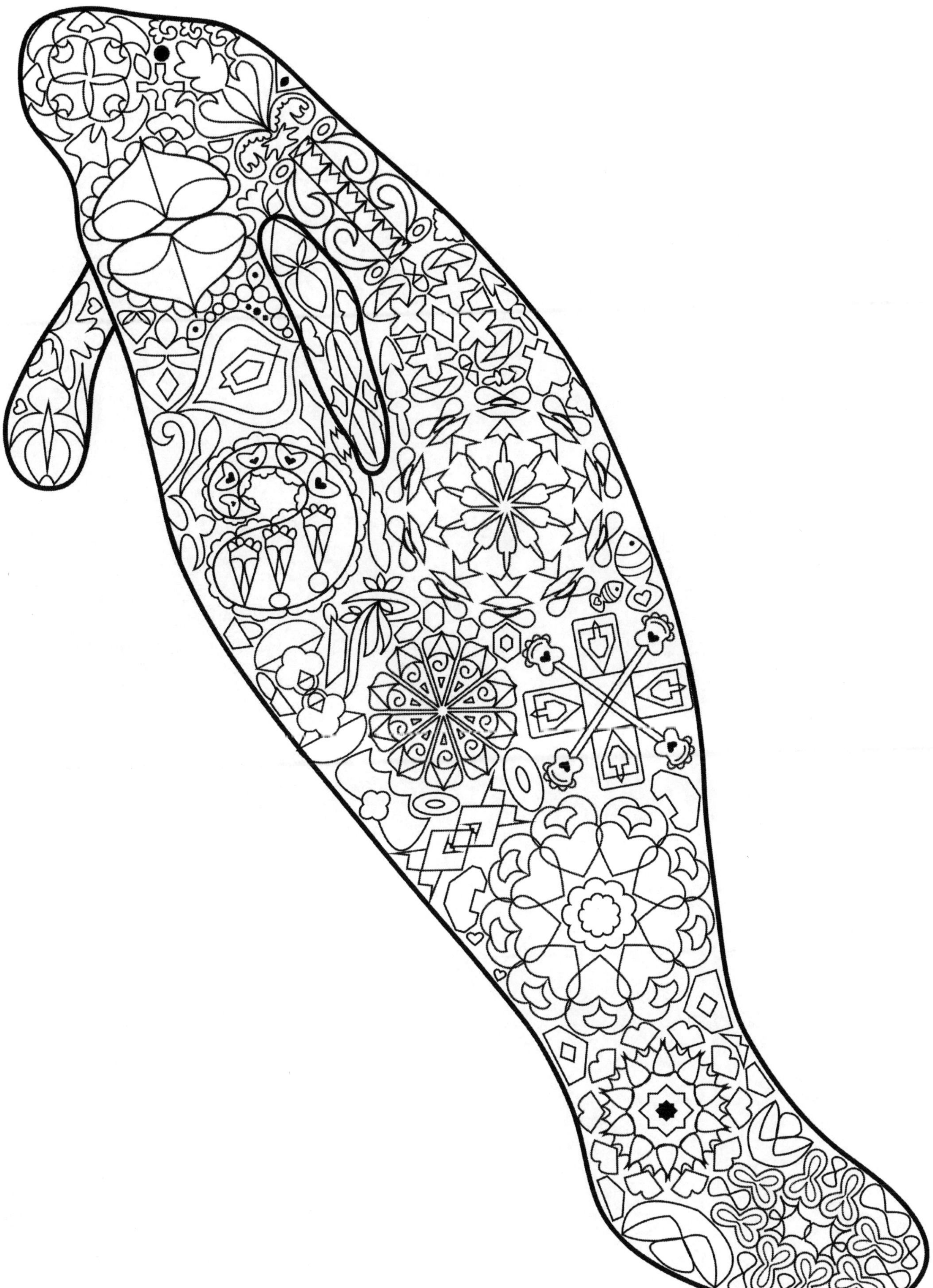

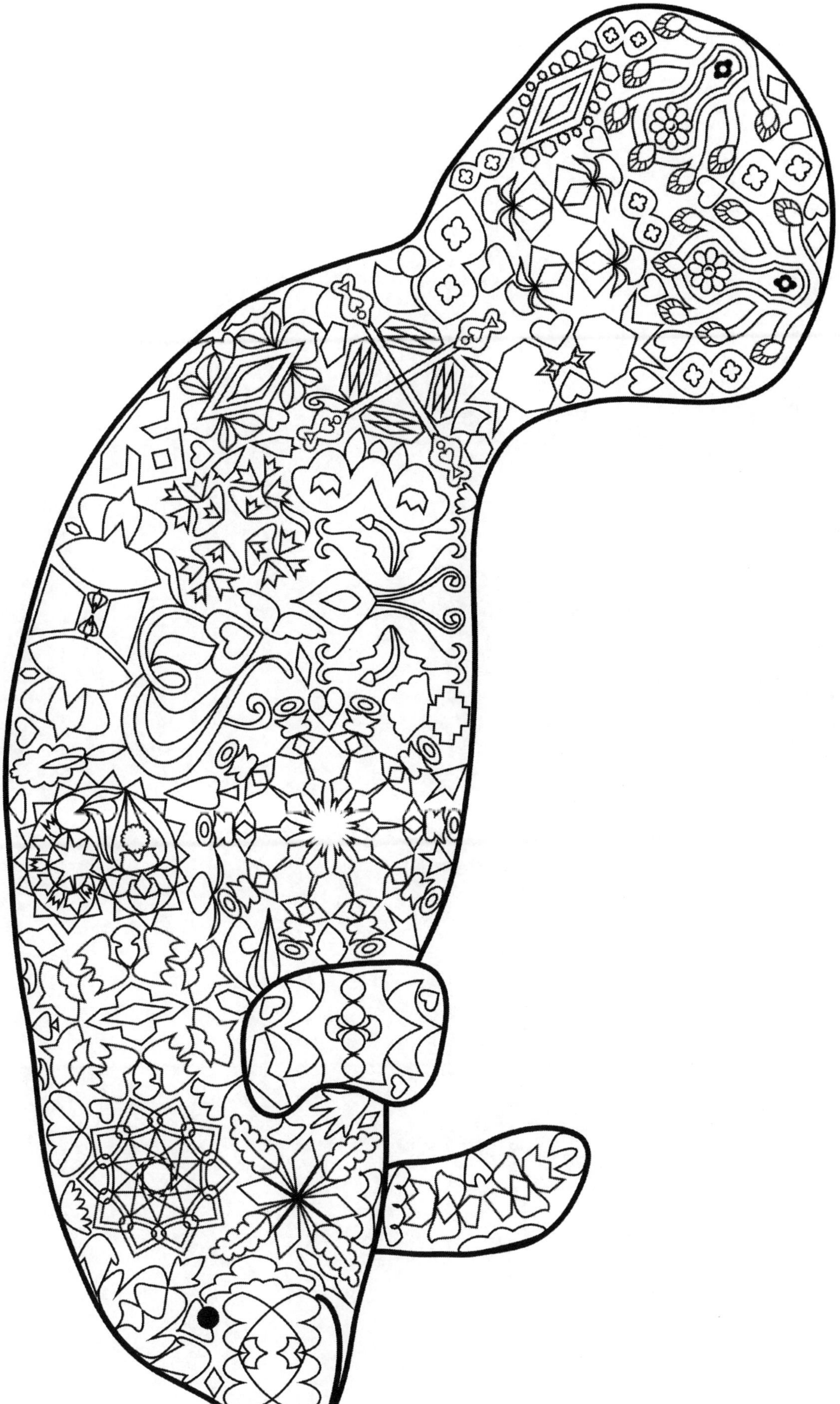

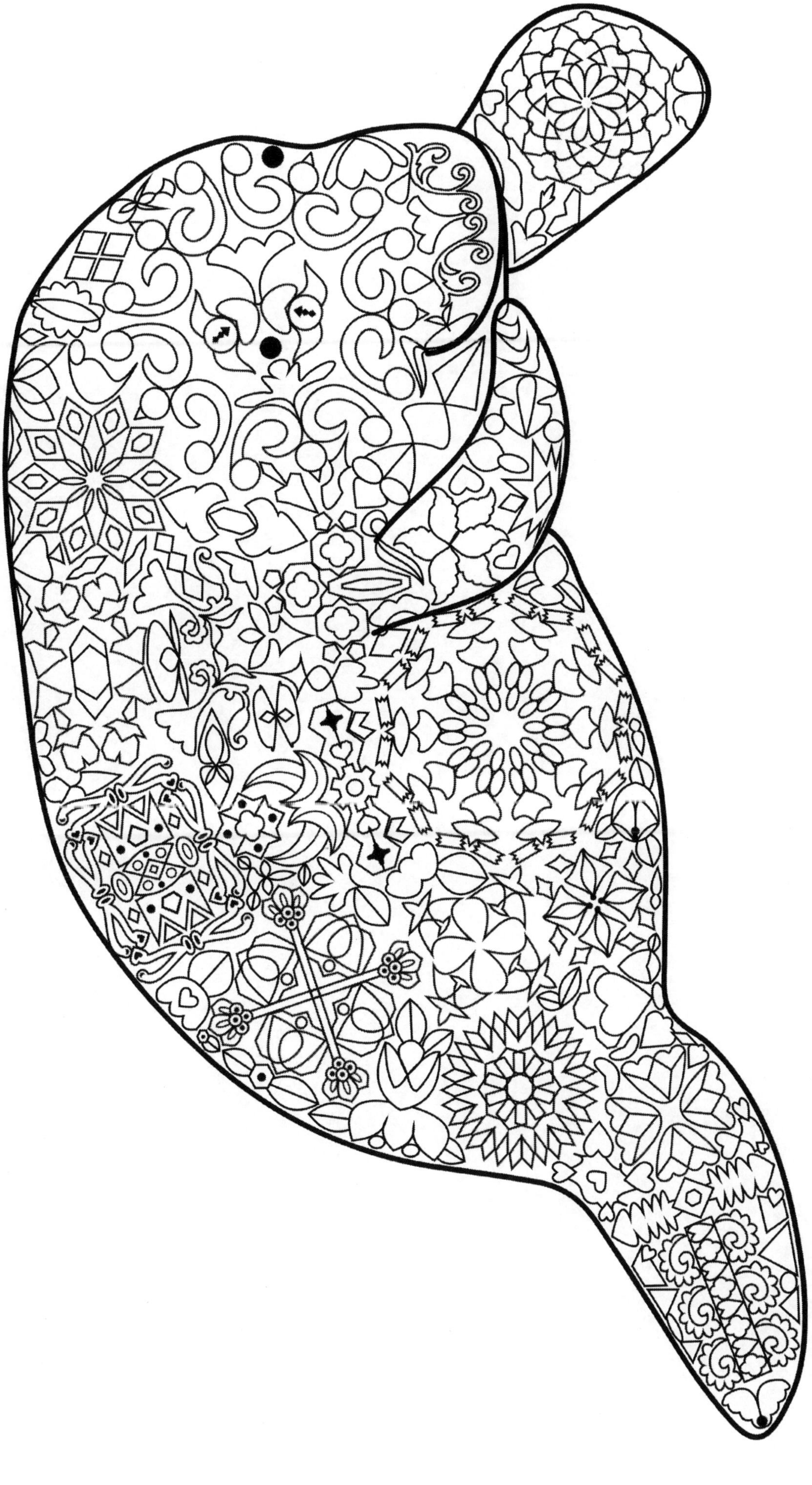

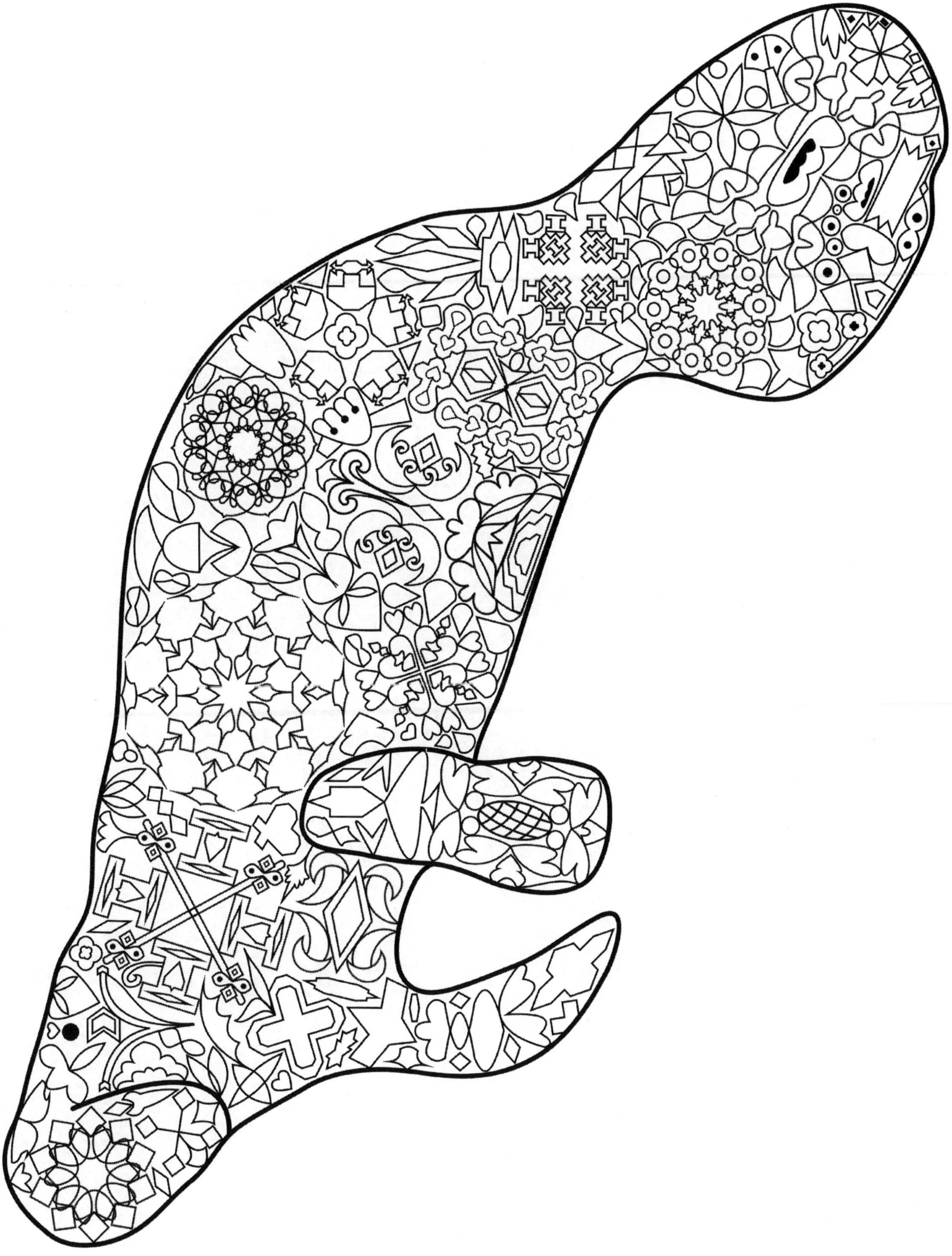

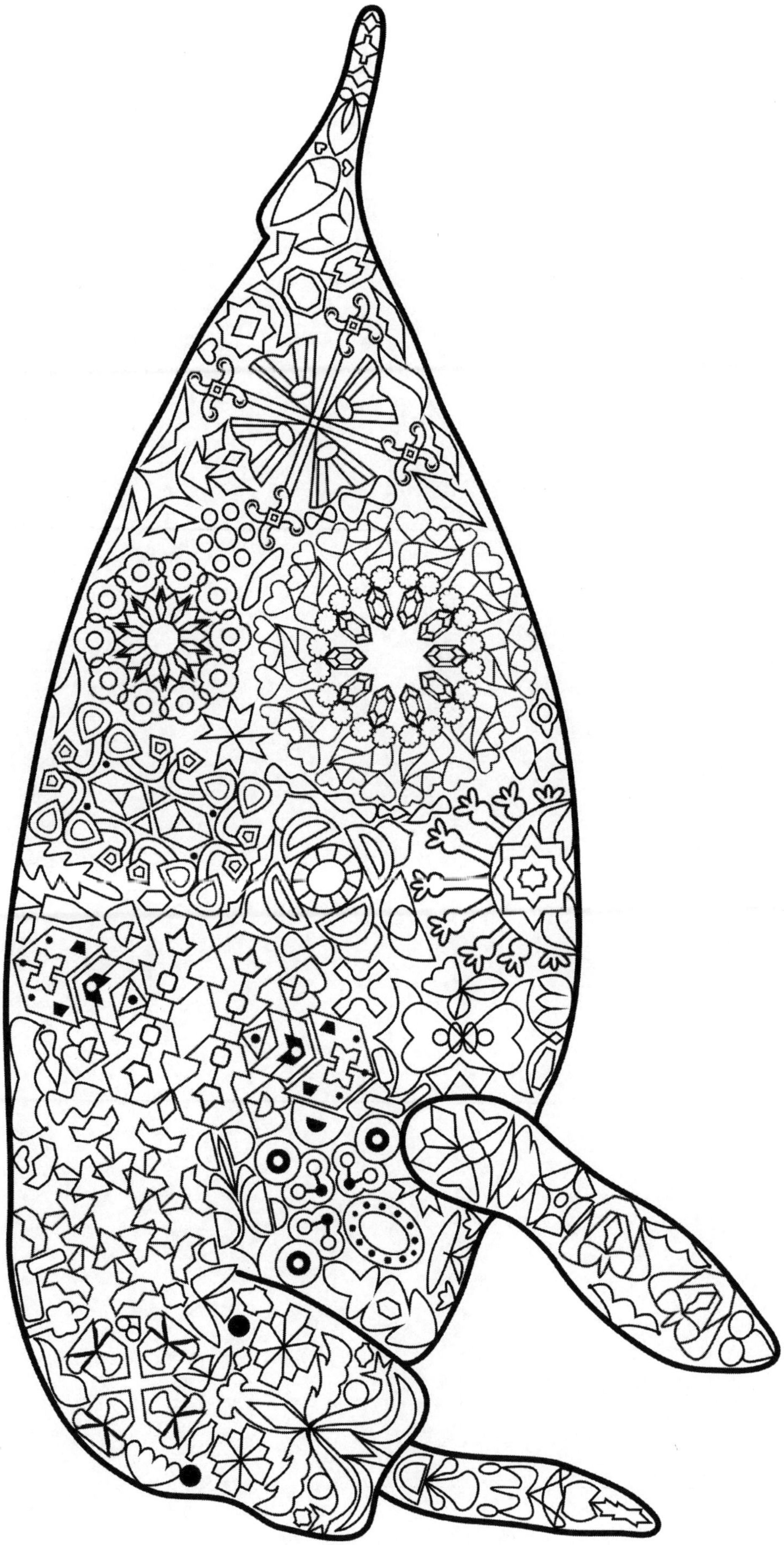

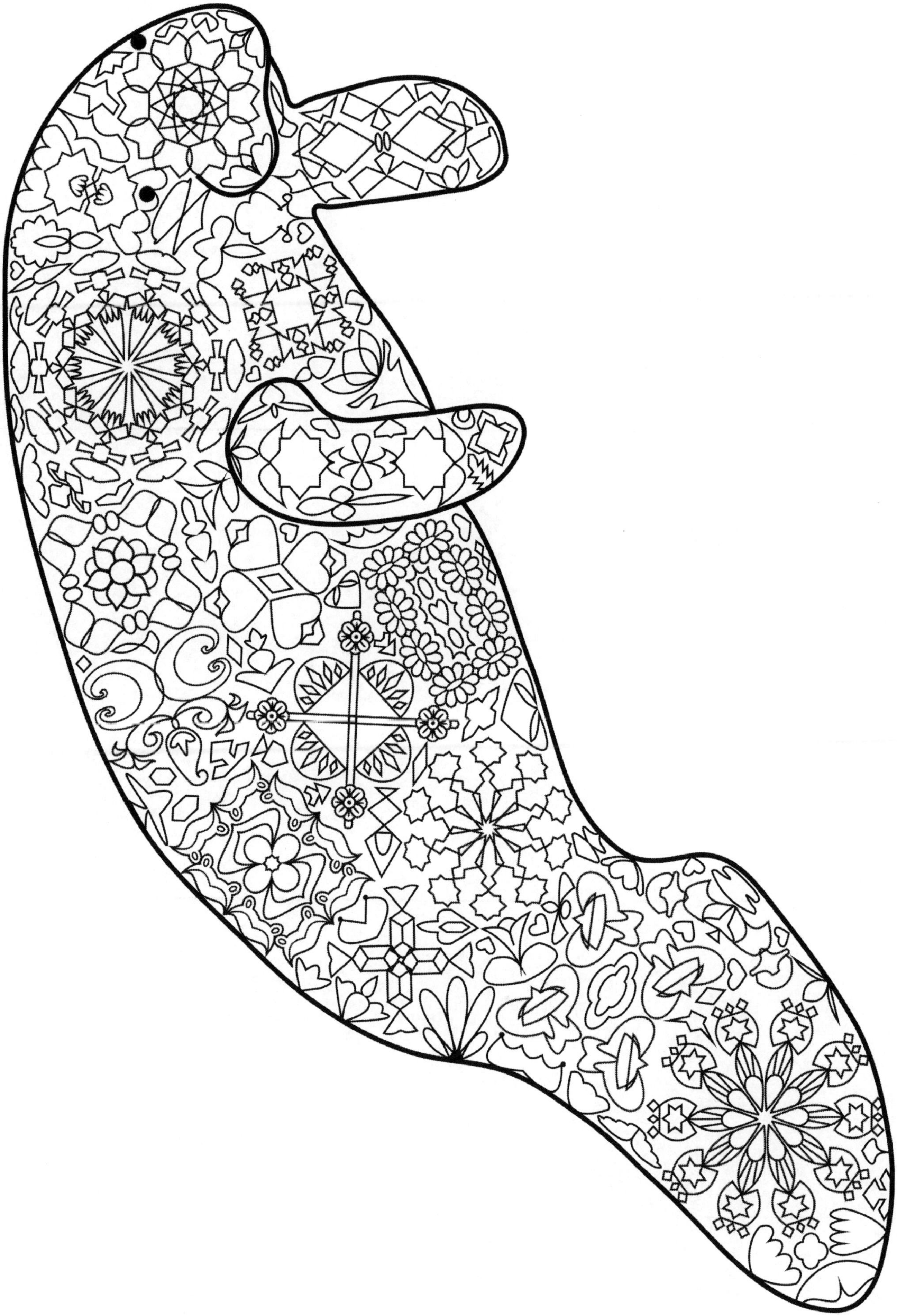

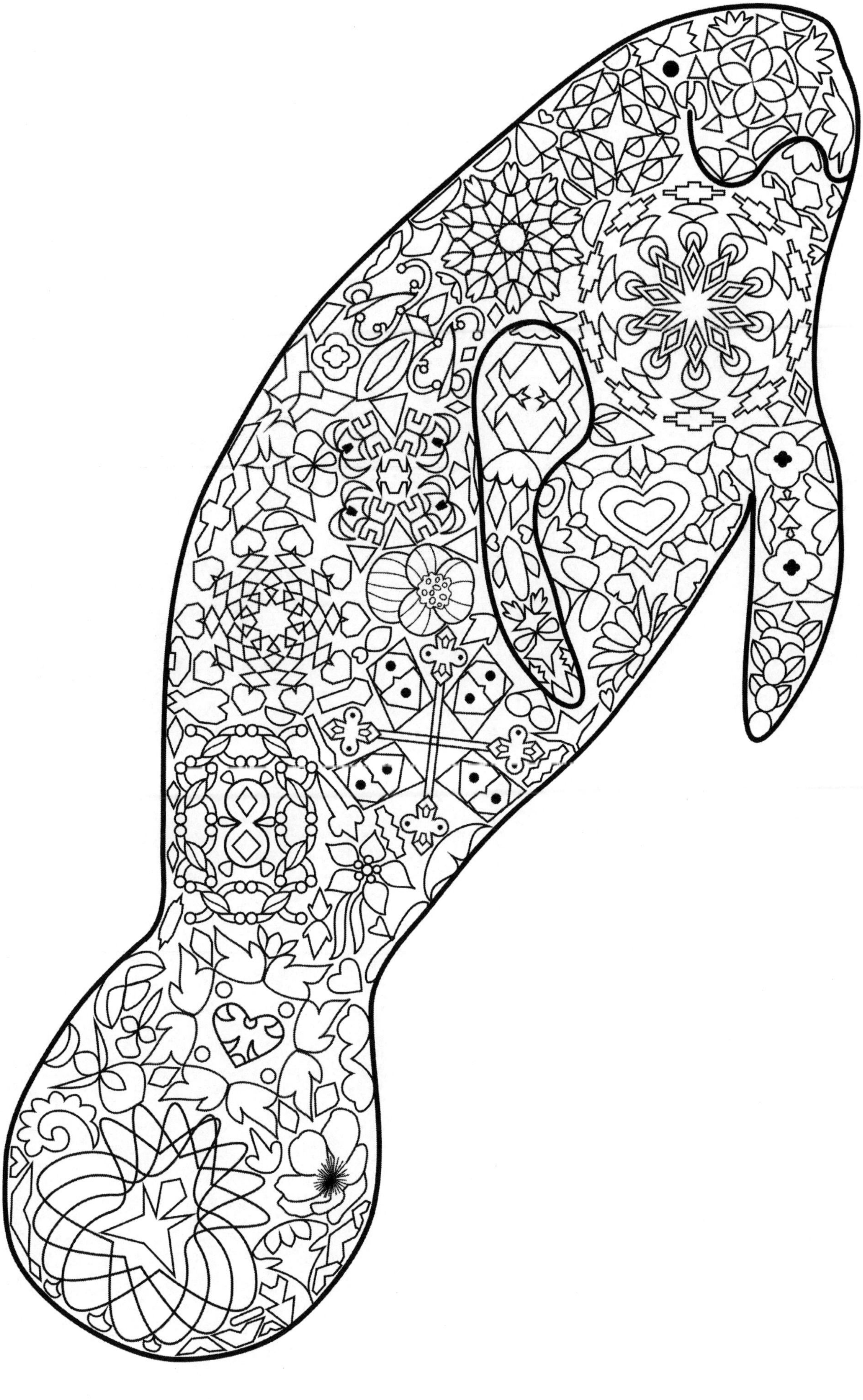

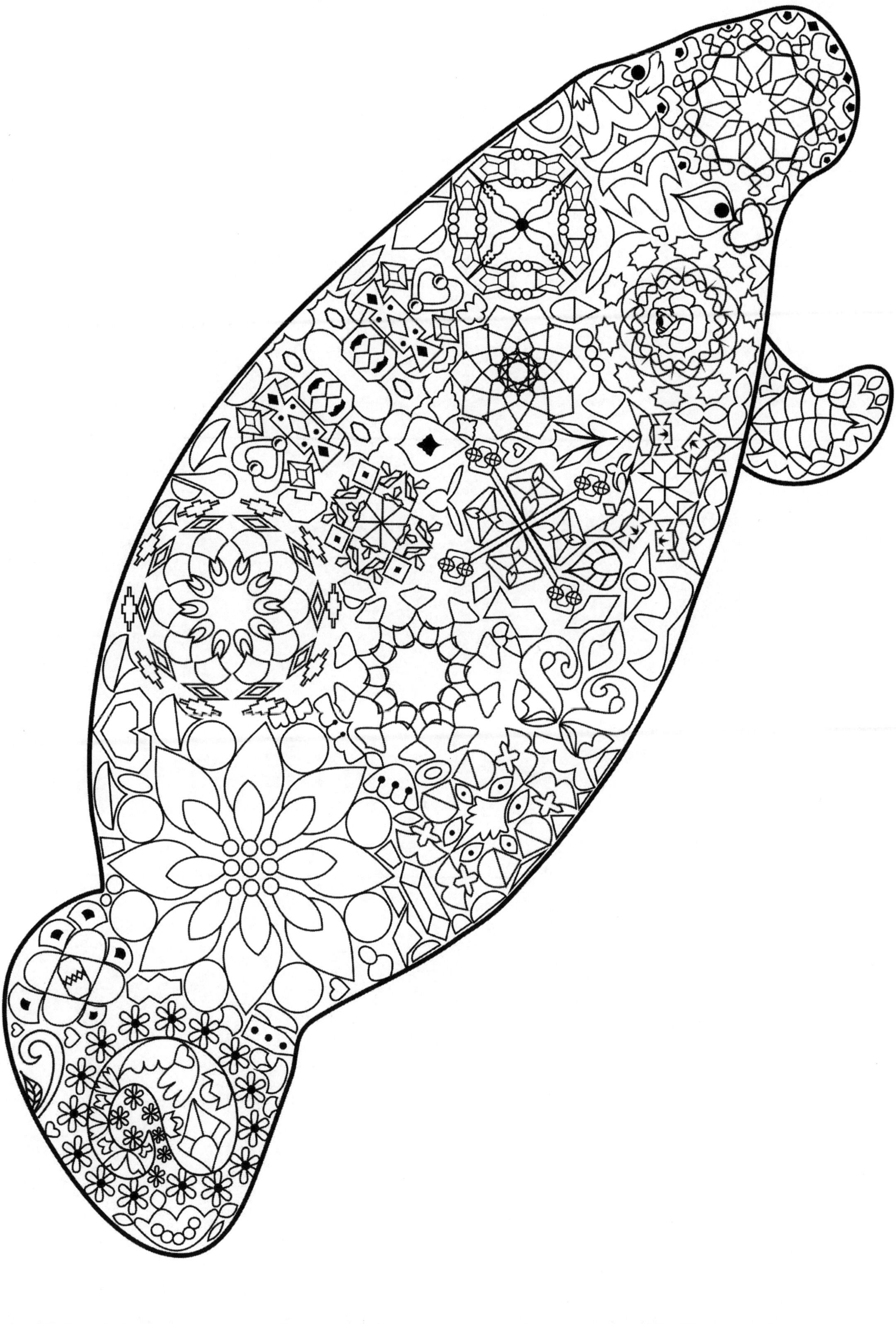

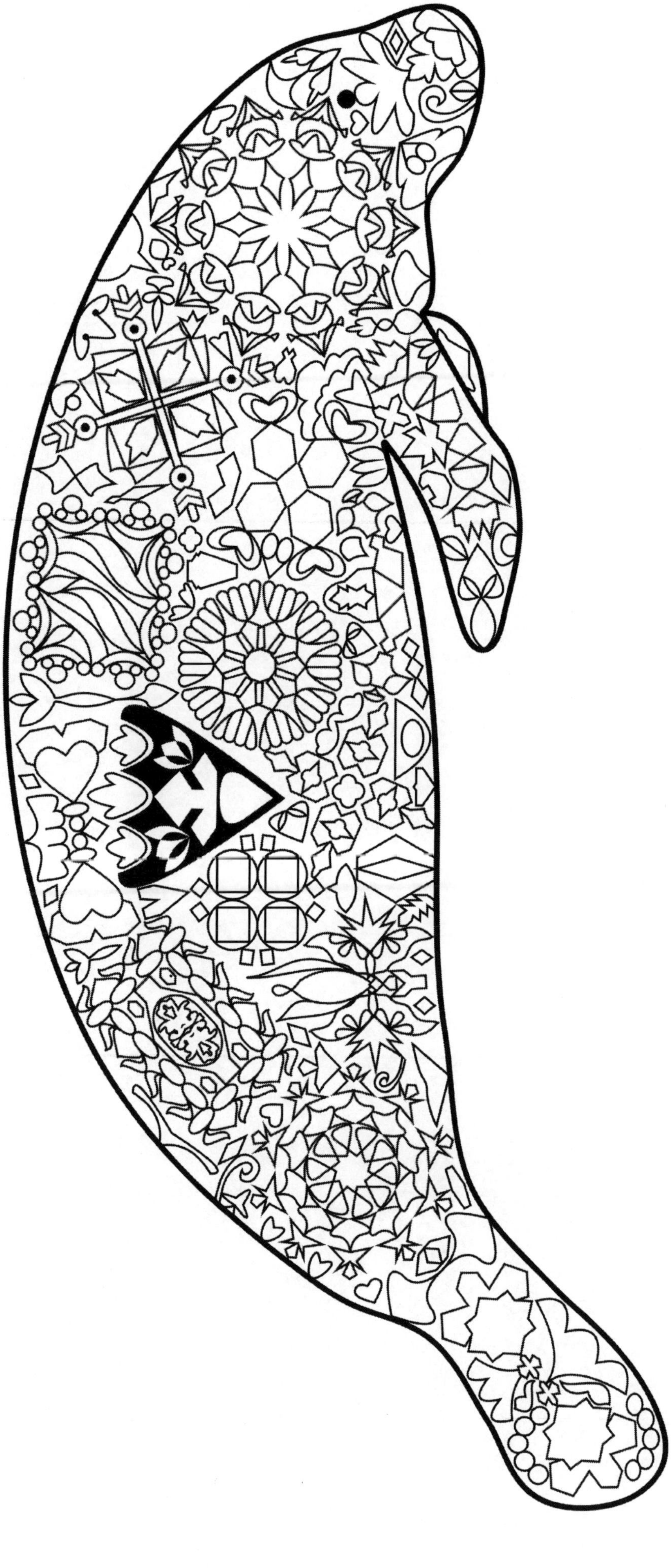

11648806R00031

Made in the USA
Lexington, KY
13 October 2018